SELECTED POEMS

DON PATERSON

Selected Poems

———

ff

faber and faber

First published in 2012
by Faber and Faber Ltd
Bloomsbury House
74–77 Great Russell Street
London WC1B 3DA

Typeset by Refinecatch Limited, Bungay, Suffolk
Printed in England by TJ International Ltd, Padstow, Cornwall

A CIP record for this book
is available from the British Library

ISBN 978–0–571–28178–7

2 4 6 8 10 9 7 5 3 1

Contents

from ORPHEUS (2006)

from RAIN (2009)

from
NIL NIL

The Ferryman's Arms

About to sit down with my half-pint of Guinness
I was magnetized by a remote phosphorescence
and drawn, like a moth, to the darkened back room
where a pool-table hummed to itself in the corner.
With ten minutes to kill and the whole place deserted
I took myself on for the hell of it. Slotting
a coin in the tongue, I looked round for a cue –
while I stood with my back turned, the balls were deposited
with an abrupt intestinal rumble; a striplight
batted awake in its dusty green cowl.
When I set down the cue-ball inside the parched D
it clacked on the slate; the nap was so threadbare
I could screw back the globe, given somewhere to stand.
As physics itself becomes something negotiable
a rash of small miracles covers the shortfall.
I went on to make an immaculate clearance.
A low punch with a wee dab of side, and the black
did the vanishing trick while the white stopped
before gently rolling back as if nothing had happened,
shouldering its way through the unpotted colours.

The boat chugged up to the little stone jetty
without breaking the skin of the water, stretching,
as black as my stout, from somewhere unspeakable
to here, where the foaming lip mussitates endlessly,
trying, with a nutter's persistence, to read
and re-read the shoreline. I got aboard early,
remembering the ferry would leave on the hour
even for only my losing opponent;
but I left him there, stuck in his tent of light, sullenly
knocking the balls in, for practice, for next time.

Morning Prayer
after Rimbaud

I spend my life sitting, like an angel at the barber's,
with a mug in one hand, fag in the other,
my froth-slabbered face in the gantry mirror
while the smoke towels me down, warm and white.

On the midden of desire, the old dreams
still hold their heat, ferment, gently ignite –
once, my heart had thrown its weight behind them
but it saps itself now, stews in its own juice.

Having stomached my thoughts like a horrible linctus
– swilled down with, oh, fifteen, twenty pints –
I am roused only by the most bitter necessities:

then, the air high with the smell of opened cedar,
I pish gloriously into the dawn skies
while below me the spattered ferns nod their assent.

Filter

Thrown out in a glittering arc
   as clear as the winterbourne,
the jug of Murphy's I threw back
   goes hissing off the stone.

Whatever I do with all the black
   is my business alone.

from Exeunt

CURTAINS

You stop at the tourist office in Aubeterre,
a columbarium of files and dockets.
She explains, while you flip through the little leaflets
about the chapel and the puppet-theatre,
that everything is boarded up till spring,
including – before you can ask – the only hotel.
A moped purrs through the unbroken drizzle.
You catch yourself checking her hands for rings.

She prepares a light supper; you chat,
her fussy diction placing words in air
like ice in water. She leads you to her room
but gets the shivers while you strip her bare;
lifting her head, you watch her pupils bloom
into the whole blue iris, then the white.

Heliographer

I thought we were sitting in the sky.
My father decoded the world beneath:
our tenement, the rival football grounds,
the long bridges, slung out across the river.
Then I gave myself a fright
with the lemonade bottle. Clunk –
the glass thread butting my teeth
as I bolted my mouth to the lip.

Naw . . . copy me. It's how the grown-ups drink.
Propped in my shaky,
single-handed grip,
I tilted the bottle towards the sun
until it detonated with light,
my lips pursed like a trumpeter's.

Sunset, Visingsö
after Jørn-Erik Berglund

The lake has simplified
to one sleep-wave
bounced between shores.

All evening,
as superstition requires,
my eyes have not left it –

the fabulous animal
I will flay for the colour
its skin grows when it dreams.

Sisters
for Eva

Back then, our well of tenements
powered the black torch that could find
the moon at midday: four hours later
the stars would be squandered on us.

*

As the sun spread on her freckled back
I felt as if I'd turned the corner
to a bright street, scattered with coins;
for weeks, I counted them over and over.

*

In a dark kitchen, my ears still burning,
I'd dump the lilo, binoculars, almanac
and close the door on the flourishing mess
of Arabic and broken lines.

*

Though she swears they're not identical
when I dropped her sister at the airport
my palms hurt as she spoke my name
and I bit my tongue back when I kissed her.

*

Nowadays, having shrunk the sky
to a skull-sized planetarium
– all fairy-lights and yawning voice-overs –
I only stay up for novae, or comets.

*

Some mornings I wake, and fantasize
I've slipped into her husband's place
as he breathes at her back, sliding his tongue
through Fomalhaut and the Southern Cross.

An Elliptical Stylus

My uncle was beaming: 'Aye, yer elliptical stylus –
fairly brings out a' the wee details.'
Balanced at a fraction of an ounce
the fat cartridge sank down like a feather;
music billowed into three dimensions
as if we could have walked between the players.

My Dad, who could appreciate the difference,
went to Largs to buy an elliptical stylus
for our ancient, beat-up Philips turntable.
We had the guy in stitches: 'You can't . . .
Er . . . you'll have to *upgrade your equipment.*'
Still smirking, he sent us from the shop
with a box of needles, thick as carpet-tacks,
the only sort they made to fit our model.

(Supposing I'd been *his* son: let's eavesdrop
on 'Fidelities', the poem I'm writing now:
The day my father died, he showed me how
he'd prime the deck for optimum performance:
it's that lesson I recall – how he'd refine
the arm's weight, to leave the stylus balanced
somewhere between ellipsis and precision,
as I gently lower the sharp nip to the line
and wait for it to pick up the vibration
till it moves across the page, like a cardiograph . . .)

We drove back slowly, as if we had a puncture;
my Dad trying not to blink, and that man's laugh
stuck in my head, which is where the story sticks,
and any attempt to cauterize this fable
with something axiomatic on the nature
of articulacy and inheritance,
since he can well afford to make his *own*
excuses, you your own interpretation.
But if you still insist on resonance –
I'd swing for him, and every other cunt
happy to let my father know his station,
which probably includes yourself. To be blunt.

Amnesia

I was, as they later confirmed, a very sick boy.
The star performer at the meeting-house,
my eyes rolled back to show the whites, my arms
outstretched in catatonic supplication
while I gibbered impeccably in the gorgeous tongues
of the aerial orders. On Tuesday nights, before
I hit the Mission, I'd nurse my little secret:
Blind Annie Spall, the dead evangelist
I'd found still dying in creditable squalor
above the fishmonger's in Rankine Street.
The room was ripe with gurry and old sweat;
from her socket in the greasy mattress, Annie
belted through hoarse chorus after chorus
while I prayed loudly, absently enlarging
the crater that I'd gouged in the soft plaster.
Her eyes had been put out before the war,
just in time to never see the daughter
with the hare-lip and the kilt of dirty dishtowels
who ran the brothel from the upstairs flat
and who'd chap to let me know my time was up,
then lead me down the dark hall, its zoo-smell,
her slippers peeling off the sticky lino.
At the door, I'd shush her quiet, pressing
my bus-fare earnestly into her hand.

Four years later. Picture me: drenched in patchouli,
strafed with hash-burns, casually arranged
on Susie's bed. Smouldering frangipani;
Dali's *The Persistence of Memory*;
pink silk loosely knotted round the lamp
to soften the light; a sheaf of Penguin Classics,
their spines all carefully broken in the middle;
a John Martyn album mumbling through the speakers.
One hand was jacked up her skirt, the other trailing
over the cool wall behind the headboard
where I found the hole in the plaster again.
The room stopped like a lift. Sue went on talking.
It was a nightmare, Don. We had to gut the place.

The Trans-Siberian Express
for Eva

One day we will make our perfect journey –
the great train smashing through Dundee, Brooklyn
and off into the endless tundra,
the earth flattening out before us.

I follow your continuous arrival,
shedding veil after veil after veil –
the automatic doors wincing away
while you stagger back from the buffet

slopping *Laphroaig* and decent coffee
until you face me from that long enfilade
of glass, stretched to vanishing point
like facing mirrors, a lifetime of days.

Wind-Tunnel

Sometimes, in autumn, the doors between the days
fall open; in any other season
this would be a dangerous mediumship
though now there is just the small exchange of air
as from one room to another. A street
becomes a faint biography: you walk
through a breath of sweetpea, pipesmoke, an old perfume.

But one morning, the voices carry from everywhere:
from the first door and the last, two whistling draughts
zero in with such unholy dispatch
you do not scorch the sheets, or wake your wife.

Poem

after Ladislav Skala

The ship pitched in the rough sea
and I could bear it no longer
so I closed my eyes
and imagined myself on a ship
in a rough sea-crossing.

The woman rose up below me
and I could bear it no longer
so I closed my eyes
and imagined myself making love
to the very same woman.

When I came into the world
I closed my eyes
and imagined my own birth.
Still
I have not opened my eyes to this world.

Bedfellows

An inch or so above the bed
   the yellow blindspot hovers
where the last incumbent's greasy head
   has worn away the flowers.

Every night I have to rest
   my head in his dead halo;
I feel his heart tick in my wrist;
   then, below the pillow,

his suffocated voice resumes
   its dreary innuendo:
there are other ways to leave the room
   than the door and the window

Nil Nil

Just as any truly accurate representation of a particular
geography can only exist on a scale of 1:1 (imagine the
vast, rustling map of Burgundy, say, settling over it like a
freshly starched sheet!) so it is with all our abandoned
histories, those ignoble lines of succession that end in
neither triumph nor disaster, but merely plunge on into
deeper and deeper obscurity; only in the infinite ghost-
libraries of the imagination – their only possible analogue
– can their ends be pursued, the dull and terrible facts
finally authenticated.

François Aussemain, *Pensées*

From the top, then, the zenith, the silent footage:
McGrandle, majestic in ankle-length shorts,
his golden hair shorn to an open book, sprinting
the length of the park for the long hoick forward,
his balletic toe-poke nearly bursting the roof
of the net; a shaky pan to the Erskine St End
where a plague of grey bonnets falls out of the clouds.
But ours is a game of two halves, and this game
the semi they went on to lose; from here
it's all down, from the First to the foot of the Second,
McGrandle, Visocchi and Spankie detaching
like bubbles to speed the descent into pitch-sharing,
pay-cuts, pawned silver, the Highland Division,
the absolute sitters ballooned over open goals,
the dismal nutmegs, the scores so obscene
no respectable journal will print them; though one day
Farquhar's spectacular bicycle-kick
will earn him a name-check in Monday's obituaries.
Besides the one setback – the spell of giant-killing

in the Cup (Lochee Violet, then Aberdeen Bon Accord,
the deadlock with Lochee Harp finally broken
by Farquhar's own-goal in the replay)
nothing inhibits the fifty-year slide
into Sunday League, big tartan flasks,
open hatchbacks parked squint behind goal-nets,
the half-time satsuma, the dog on the pitch,
then the Boys' Club, sponsored by Skelly Assurance,
then Skelly Dry Cleaners, then nobody;
stud-harrowed pitches with one-in-five inclines,
grim fathers and perverts with Old English Sheepdogs
lining the touch, moaning softly.
Now the unrefereed thirty-a-sides,
terrified fat boys with callipers minding
four jackets on infinite, notional fields;
ten years of dwindling, half-hearted kickabouts
leaves two little boys – Alastair Watt,
who answers to 'Forty', and wee Horace Madden,
so smelly the air seems to quiver above him –
playing desperate two-touch with a bald tennis ball
in the hour before lighting-up time.
Alastair cheats, and goes off with the ball
leaving wee Horace to hack up a stone
and dribble it home in the rain;
past the stopped swings, the dead shanty-town
of allotments, the black shell of Skelly Dry Cleaners
and into his cul-de-sac, where, accidentally,
he neatly back-heels it straight into the gutter
then tries to swank off like he meant it.

Unknown to him, it is all that remains
of a lone fighter-pilot, who, returning at dawn
to find Leuchars was not where he'd left it,
took time out to watch the Sidlaws unsheathed
from their great black tarpaulin, the haar burn off Tayport
and Venus melt into Carnoustie, igniting
the shoreline; no wind, not a cloud in the sky
and no one around to admire the discretion
of his unscheduled exit: the engine plopped out
and would not re-engage, sending him silently
twirling away like an ash-key,
his attempt to bail out only partly successful,
yesterday having been April the 1st –
the ripcord unleashing a flurry of socks
like a sackful of doves rendered up to the heavens
in private irenicon. He caught up with the plane
on the ground, just at the instant the tank blew
and made nothing of him, save for his fillings,
his tackets, his lucky half-crown and his gallstone,
now anchored between the steel bars of a stank
that looks to be biting the bullet on this one.

In short, this is where you get off, reader;
I'll continue alone, on foot, in the failing light,
following the trail as it steadily fades
into road-repairs, birdsong, the weather, nirvana,
the plot thinning down to a point so refined
not even the angels could dance on it. Goodbye.

from
GOD'S GIFT TO WOMEN

Addenda

Scott Paterson, b. – d. Oct. '65

(i)

The Gellyburn is six feet under;
they sunk a pipe between its banks,
tricked it in and turfed it over.
We heard it rush from stank to stank,
Ardler Wood to the Caird Estate.

Scott said when you crossed the river
you saw sparks; if you ran at it
something snagged on the line of water.

(ii)

It was Scott who found the one loose knot
from the thousand dead eyes in the fence,
and inside, the tiny silver lochan
with lilies, green rushes, and four swans.
A true artist, he set his pitch:

uncorking the little show for tuppence
he'd count a minute on his watch
while a boy set his eye to the light.

(iii)

One week he was early, and turned up
at the Foot Clinic in Kemback Street
to see a little girl parade
before the Indian doctor, stripped
down to just her underthings.

Now he dreams about her every night
working through his stretches: *The Mermaid;*
The Swan; The Tightrope-Walker; Wings.

(iv)

They leave the party, arm in arm
to a smore so thick, her voice comes
to him as if from a small room;
their footprints in the creaking snow
the love-pact they affirm and reaffirm.

Open for fags, the blazing kiosk
crowns old Jock in asterisks.
He is a saint, and Scott tells him so.

00:00: Law Tunnel

leased to the Scottish Mushroom Company
after its closure in 1927

(i)

In the airy lull
between the wars
they cut the rails
and closed the doors

on the stalled freight:
crate on crate
of blood and earth –
the shallow berth

of the innocents,
their long room
stale and tense
with the same dream

(ii)

Strewn among
the ragged queue –
the snoring king
and his retinue,

Fenrir, Pol Pot,
Captain Oates
and the leprechauns –
are the teeth, the bones

[25]

and begging-cup
of the drunken piper.
The rats boiled up
below the sleepers

(iii)

The crippled boy
of Hamelin
pounds away
at the locked mountain

waist-deep in thorn
and all forlorn,
he tries to force
the buried doors

I will go to my mother
and sing of my shame
I will grow up to father
the race of the lame

from 1001 Nights: The Early Years

The male muse is paid in silences. Shahrāzād could not have been bought for less than a minor Auschwitz.

Erszébet Szanto

Dawn, and I woke up grieving for my arm
long dead below the little drunken carcass
still shut in her drunk dream. In mine, I recall,
I was fixing a stamp in a savings-book, half-full
of the same heavenly profile, a vast harem
of sisters, each one day younger than the last . . .

Heaven, to bed the same new wife each night!
And I try; but morning always brings her back
changed, although I recognise the room:
my puddled suit, her dog-eared Kerouac,
the snot-stream of a knotted Fetherlite
draped on the wineglass. I killed the alarm,

then took her head off with the kitchen knife
and no more malice than I might a rose
for my daily buttonhole. One hand, like a leaf,
still flutters in half-hearted valediction.
I am presently facing the wall, nose-to-nose
with Keanu Reeves. It is a sad reflection.

The Scale of Intensity

1) Not felt. Smoke still rises vertically. In sensitive individuals, déjà vu, mild amnesia. Sea like a mirror.

2) Detected by persons at rest or favourably placed, i.e. in upper floors, hammocks, cathedrals, etc. Leaves rustle.

3) Light sleepers wake. Glasses chink. Hairpins, paperclips display slight magnetic properties. Irritability. Vibration like passing of light trucks.

4) Small bells ring. Small increase in surface tension and viscosity of certain liquids. Domestic violence. Furniture overturned.

5) Heavy sleepers wake. Pendulum clocks stop. Public demonstrations. Large flags fly. Vibration like passing of heavy trucks.

6) Large bells ring. Bookburning. Aurora visible in daylight hours. Unprovoked assaults on strangers. Glassware broken. Loose tiles fly from roof.

7) Weak chimneys broken off at roofline. Waves on small ponds, water turbid with mud. Unprovoked assaults on neighbours. Large static charges built up on windows, mirrors, television screens.

8) Perceptible increase in weight of stationary objects: books, cups, pens heavy to lift. Fall of stucco and some masonry. Systematic rape of women and young girls. Sand craters. Cracks in wet ground.

9) Small trees uprooted. Bathwater drains in reverse vortex. Wholesale slaughter of religious and ethnic minorities. Conspicuous cracks in ground. Damage to reservoirs and underground pipelines.

10) Large trees uprooted. Measurable tide in puddles, teacups, etc. Torture and rape of small children. Irreparable damage to foundations. Rails bend. Sand shifts horizontally on beaches.

11) Standing impossible. Widespread self-mutilation. Corposant visible on pylons, lampposts, metal railings. Waves seen on ground surface. Most bridges destroyed.

12) Damage total. Movement of hour hand perceptible. Large rock masses displaced. Sea white.

11:00: Baldovan

Base Camp. Horizontal sleet. Two small boys
have raised the steel flag of the 20 terminus:

me and Ross Mudie are going up the Hilltown
for the first time ever on our own.

I'm weighing up my spending power: the shillings,
tanners, black pennies, florins with bald kings,

the cold blazonry of a half-crown, threepenny bits
like thick cogs, making them chank together in my
   pockets.

I plan to buy comics,
sweeties, and magic tricks.

However, I am obscurely worried, as usual,
over matters of procedure, the protocol of travel,

and keep asking Ross the same questions:
where we should sit, when to pull the bell, even

if we have enough money for the fare,
whispering, *Are ye sure? Are ye sure?*

I cannot know the little good it will do me;
the bus will let us down in another country

with the wrong streets and streets that suddenly forget
their names at crossroads or in building-sites

and where no one will have heard of the sweets we ask for
and the man will shake the coins from our fists onto the counter

and call for his wife to come through, come through and
    see this
and if we ever make it home again, the bus

will draw into the charred wreck of itself
and we will enter the land at the point we left off

only our voices sound funny and all the houses are gone
and the rain tastes like kelly and black waves fold in

very slowly at the foot of Macalpine Road
and our sisters and mothers are fifty years dead.

Les Six

(i)

with Cocteau (far left); Georges Auric was briefly sent
to Coventry following the 'umbrella' incident.

(ii)

with Cocteau (second from the left), in the 'Chinese'
parlour, *chez* Laloy. One assumes that Poulenc sneezed.

(iii)

with Cocteau (centre left): the six friends share a joke
at de Beaumont's. Honegger obscured by his own pipe-smoke.

(iv)

with Cocteau (centre right), May '31. Absent
is Tailleferre, by this time heavily *enceinte*.

(v)

with Cocteau (under piano), rehearsing for *Lilith*,
Milhaud having failed to return from Hammersmith.

(vi)

with Cocteau (far right): late-night horseplay at *Le Boeuf*.
Durey is represented by his photograph.

A Private Bottling

*So I will go, then. I would rather grieve over your absence
than over you.*
Antonio Porchia

Back in the same room that an hour ago
we had led, lamp by lamp, into the darkness
I sit down and turn the radio on low
as the last girl on the planet still awake
reads a dedication to the ships
and puts on a recording of the ocean.

I carefully arrange a chain of nips
in a big fairy-ring; in each square glass
the tincture of a failed geography,
its dwindled burns and woodlands, whin-fires, heather,
the sklent of its wind and its salty rain,
the love-worn habits of its working-folk,
the waveform of their speech, and by extension
how they sing, make love, or take a joke.

So I have a good nose for this sort of thing.

Then I will suffer kiss after fierce kiss
letting their gold tongues slide along my tongue
as each gives up, in turn, its little song
of the patient years in glass and sherry-oak,
the shy negotiations with the sea,
air and earth, the trick of how the peat-smoke
was shut inside it, like a black thought.

Tonight I toast her with the extinct malts
of Ardlussa, Ladyburn and Dalintober
and an ancient pledge of passionate indifference:
Ochon o do dhóigh mé mo chlairsach ar a shon,
wishing her health, as I might wish her weather.

When the circle is closed and I have drunk myself sober
I will tilt the blinds a few degrees, and watch
the dawn grow in a glass of liver-salts,
wait for the birds, the milk-float's sweet nothings,
then slip back to the bed where she lies curled,
replace the live egg of her burning ass
gently, in the cold nest of my lap,
as dead to her as she is to the world.

*

Here we are again; it is precisely
twelve, fifteen, thirty years down the road
and one turn higher up the spiral chamber
that separates the burnt ale and dark grains
of what I know, from what I can remember.
Now each glass holds its micro-episode
in permanent suspension, like a movie-frame
on acetate, until it plays again,
revivified by a suave connoisseurship
that deepens in the silence and the dark
to something like an infinite sensitivity.
This is no romantic fantasy: my father
used to know a man who'd taste the sea,
then leave his nets strung out along the bay
because there were no fish in it that day.

Everything is in everything else. It is a matter
of attunement, as once, through the hiss and backwash,
I steered the dial into the voice of God
slightly to the left of Hilversum,
half-drowned by some big, blurry waltz
the way some stars obscure their dwarf companions
for centuries, till someone thinks to look.

In the same way, I can isolate the feints
of feminine effluvia, carrion, shite,
those rogues and toxins only introduced
to give the composition a little weight
as rough harmonics do the violin-note
or Pluto, Cheiron and the lesser saints
might do to our lives, for all you know.
(By Christ, you would recognise their absence
as anyone would testify, having sunk
a glass of *North British,* run off a patent still
in some sleet-hammered satellite of Edinburgh:
a bleak spirit no amount of caramel
could sweeten or disguise, its after-effect
somewhere between a blanket-bath and a sad wank.
There is, no doubt, a bar in Lothian
where it is sworn upon and swallowed neat
by furloughed riggers and the Special Police,
men who hate the company of women.)

O whiskies of Long Island and Provence!
This little number catches at the throat
but is all sweetness in the finish: my tongue trips

first through burning brake-fluid, then nicotine,
pastis, *Diorissimo* and wet grass;
another is silk sleeves and lip-service
with a kick like a smacked puss in a train-station;
another, the light charge and the trace of zinc
tap-water picks up at the moon's eclipse.
You will know the time I mean by this.

Because your singular absence, in your absence,
has bred hard, tonight I take the waters
with the whole clan: our faceless ushers, bridesmaids,
our four Shelties, three now ghosts of ghosts;
our douce sons and our lovely loudmouthed daughters
who will, by this late hour, be fully grown,
perhaps with unborn children of their own.
So finally, let me propose a toast:
not to love, or life, or real feeling,
but to their sentimental residue;
to your sweet memory, but not to you.

The sun will close its circle in the sky
before I close my own, and drain the purely
offertory glass that tastes of nothing
but silence, burnt dust on the valves, and whisky.

The End

At round about four months or so
– the time is getting shorter –
I look down as the face below
goes sliding underwater

and though I know it's over with
and she is miles from me
I stay a while to mine the earth
for what was lost at sea

as if the faces of the drowned
might turn up in the harrow:
hold me when I hold you down
and plough the lonely furrow

God's Gift to Women

'The man seems to be under the impression he is God's gift to
womankind,' said Arthur. Cradling the enormous, rancid bunch
of stock he had brought her, Mary reflected that the Holy Father
could no more be depended upon to make an appropriate donation
than any other representative of His sex.
    G. K. Chesterton, 'Gabriel Gale and the Pearl Necklace'

Dundee, and the Magdalen Green.
The moon is staring down the sun;
one last white javelin inches out
of Lucklawhill, and quietly floats
to JFK or Reykjavik.
Newport comes on with a click
like the door-light from an opened fridge.
The coal train shivers on the bridge.

The east wind blows into his fist;
the bare banks rise up, thigh and breast;
half-blue, cursing under her breath,
the muddy Venus of the Firth
lunges through the waterburn.
You come: I wish the wind would turn
so your face would stay like this,
your lips drawn up to blow a kiss

even now, at your martyrdom –
the window, loose inside its frame,
rolls like a drum, but at the last
gives out, and you give up the ghost.
Meanwhile, our vernacular
Atlantis slides below the stars:
My Lord's Bank, Carthagena, Flisk
go one by one into the dusk.

So here we lie, babes in the wood
of voluntary orphanhood,
left in the dark to bleat and shiver
in my leaf-pattern duvet-cover,
and where Jakob or Wilhelm ought to
stencil in the fatal motto
your bandage has unscrolled above
our tousled heads. Still, we survive –

although, for years, the doctors led
us back along the trail of bread
as if it ran to our rebirth,
not our stepmother's frozen hearth;
when they'd gone, she'd take us back
with big rocks in our haversacks
and twice as far in as before.
But I keep coming back for more,

and every second Wednesday
rehearse the aetiology
of this, my current all-time low
at twenty-seven quid a throw.
Ten years drawing out the sting
have ascertained the following:
a model of precocity –
Christ at one year, Cain at three

(a single blow was all it took;
the fucker died inside a week) –
I'd wed my mother long before
she'd think to lock the bathroom door,
as much a sly move to defraud
my father of his fatherhood
as clear the blood-debt with the gift
of my right hand; with my left

I dealt myself the whole estate
and in the same stroke, wiped the slate
of my own inheritance. Anyway,
as the semi-bastard progeny
of a morganatic union
(the Mother ranks below the Son),
I am the first man and the last:
there will be no title or bequest.

Once, to my own disbelief,
I almost took a second wife,
and came so close that others slurred
our names together as one word,
a word she gave, a word I took,
a word she conjured with, and broke.
So I filled the diary up again
with the absences of other men:

John's overtime, Jack's training-course,
returning in the tiny hours
with my head clear as a bullet-hole
and a Durex wrapped in toilet roll,
the operation so risk-free
I'd take my own seed home with me
and bury it deep down in the trash,
beside the bad fruit and the ash.

Thus the cross laid on my shoulder
grew light, as I grew harder, colder,
and in each subsequent affair
became the cross that others bear.
Until last night, when I found pain
enough to fill the stony grain
with that old yearly hurt, as if
I might yet burst back into leaf –

O my dear, my 'delicate cutter'
pale phlebotomist, blood-letter –
the back of one, I came home drunk
to find you standing at the sink,
the steady eye of your own storm
feathering up your white forearm
with the edge of a Bic Ladyshave
and the nonchalance of a Chinese chef –

next month, when the scars have gone,
we'll raid the bank and hit the town,
you in that black silk dress, cut low
enough to show an inch or so
of the opalescent hand-long scar
on your left breast. Your mother swore
that fumbling along the shelf,
you'd pulled the pan down on yourself;

but we could see her tipping out
the kettle in the carry-cot,
one eyebrow arched above your cries
as she watched the string of blisters rise
to the design that in ten years
would mark you her inferior,
when all it did was make the one
more lovely than its own dear twin,

as if some angel'd shot his come
as bright as lit magnesium
across your body as you slept.
And as you lie here, tightly happed
in the track-marked arms of Morpheus,
I only wish that I could wish
you more than luck as you delay
before that white-gloved croupier

who offers you the fanned-out pack:
a face-card. The fey and sleekit jack.
The frame yawns to a living-room.
Slim Whitman warbles through the hum
of a bad earth. The Green Lady cries
over the scene: you, compromised,
steadily drawing out the juice
of the one man you could not seduce,

but his legs are sliding up his shorts,
his mouth drops open in its slot
and at the point you suss his groans
come not from his throat but your own,
it all goes monochrome, and segues
into the usual territory.
You get up from your knees, nineteen,
half-pissed, bleeding through your jeans.

Titless, doll-eyed, party-frocked,
your mother, ashen with the shock
at this, the regular outrage,
pretends to phone the orphanage,
gets out your blue valise, and packs
it tight with pants and ankle-socks
and a pony-book to pass the time
on the long ride to the Home.

And then the old routine: frogmarched
outside to the freezing porch,
you'd shiver out the hour until
she'd shout you in and make the call.
But in your dreams they always come,
the four huge whitecoats, masked and dumb
with their biros, clipboards and pink slips,
the little gibbet of the drip,

the quilted coat with one long arm,
the napkin soaked in chloroform,
the gag, the needle and the van
that fires you down the endless lane
that ends in mile-high chicken-wire
around the silent compound, where
a tower-guard rolls a searchlight beam
over the crematorium –

Enough. Let's hold you in your dream,
leave the radio-alarm
mid-digit and unreadable,
under the bare bulb in the hall
one cranefly braced against the air,
the rain stalled like a chandelier
above the roof, the moon sandbanked
in Gemini. I have to think.

Now. Let us carefully assay
that lost soteriology
which holds Christ died to free himself,
or who slays the dragon or the wolf
on the stage of his presexual
rescue fantasy, makes the kill
not just for her flushed gratitude
but for his Father in the gods:

somewhere between His lofty blessing
and the virgin bride's undressing
the light streams from the gates of heaven
and all is promised and forgiven.
Time and again I blow the dust
off this wee psychodrama, just
a new face in the victim's role –
convinced if I can save her soul

I'll save my own. It doesn't work.
Whatever difference I make
to anyone by daylight is
dispatched in that last torpid kiss
at the darkening crossroads; from there
they go back to their torturers.
But if I could put the sleep I lose
over you to better use,

I'd work the nights as signalman
to your bad dreams, wait for that drawn-
sword sound and the blue wheelsparks,
then make the switch before the track
flicks left, and curves away to hell . . .
This once I can, and so I will.
The death-camp gates are swinging to
to let you leave, not swallow you.

They set you down upon a hill.
Your case is huge. Your hands are small.
The sun opens its golden eye
into the blue room of the sky.
A black mare nods up to your side. You
take her reins, and let her guide you
over the sky-blue, trackless heather
to the hearth, the Home, your real mother.

The Lover

after Propertius

Poor mortals, with your horoscopes and blood-tests –
what hope is there for you? Even if the plane
lands you safely, why should you not return
to your home in flames or ruins, your wife absconded,
the children blind and dying in their cots?
Even sitting quiet in a locked room
the perils are infinite and unforeseeable.
Only the lover walks upon the earth
careless of what the fates prepare for him:

so you step out at the lights, almost as if
you half-know that today you are the special one.
The woman in the windshield lifting away
her frozen cry, a white mask on a stick,
reveals herself as grey-eyed Atropos;
the sun leaves like a rocket; the sky goes out;
the road floods and widens; on the distant kerb
the lost souls groan and mew like sad trombones;
the ambulance glides up with its black sail –

when somewhere in the other world, she fills
your name full of her breath again, and at once
you float to your feet: the dark rose on your shirt
folds itself away, and you slip back
into the crowd, who, being merely human,
must remember nothing of this incident.
Just one flea-ridden dog chained to the railings,
who might be Cerberus, or patient Argos,
looks on, knowing the great law you have flouted.

Imperial

Is it normal to get this wet? Baby, I'm frightened –
I covered her mouth with my own;
she lay in my arms till the storm-window brightened
and stood at our heads like a stone

After months of jaw jaw, determined that neither
win ground, or be handed the edge,
we gave ourselves up, one to the other
like prisoners over a bridge

and no trade was ever so fair or so tender;
so where was the flaw in the plan,
the night we lay down on the flag of surrender
and woke on the flag of Japan

On Going to Meet a Zen Master in the Kyushu Mountains and Not Finding Him

for A.G.

from Advice to Young Husbands

No one slips into the same woman twice:
heaven is the innocence of its beholding.

From stroke to stroke, we exchange one bliss
wholly for another. Imagine the unfolding
river-lotus, how it duplicates
the singular perfection of itself
through the packed bud of its billion petticoats,
and your cock, here, the rapt and silent witness,
as disbelief flowers from his disbelief.

Heaven is the innocence of its beholding:
no man slips into the same woman twice.

14:50: Rosekinghall

The next train on Platform 6 will be the 14:50
Rosekinghall – Gallowshill and Blindwell, calling at:

Fairygreen – Templelands – Stars of Forthneth – Silverwells –
Honeyhole – Bee Cott – Pleasance – Sunnyblink –
Butterglen – Heatheryhaugh – St Bride's Ring – Diltie Moss –
Silvie – Leyshade – Bourtreebush – Little Fithie –
Dusty Drum – Spiral Wood – Wandershiell – Windygates –
Red Roofs – Ark Hill – Egypt – Formal –
Letter – Laverockhall – Windyedge – Catchpenny –
Framedrum – Drumtick – Little Fardle – Packhorse –
Carrot – Clatteringbrigs – Smyrna – Bucklerheads –
Outfield – Jericho – Horn – Roughstones –
Loak – Skitchen – Sturt – Oathlaw –
Wolflaw – Farnought – Drunkendubs – Stronetic –
Ironharrow Well – Goats – Tarbrax – Dameye –
Dummiesholes – Caldhame – Hagmuir – Slug of Auchrannie –
Baldragon – Thorn – Wreaths – Spurn Hill –
Drowndubs – The Bloody Inches – Halfway – Groan,
where the train will divide

Candlebird*

after Abbas Ibn Al-Ahnaf, c.750

If, tonight, she scorns me for my song,
You may be sure of this: within the year
Another man will say this verse to her
And she will yield to him for its sad sweetness.

' *"Then I am like the candlebird,"* ' he'll continue,
After explaining what a candlebird is,
' *"Whose lifeless eyes see nothing and see all,*
Lighting their small room with my burning tongue;

His shadow rears above hers on the wall
As hour by hour, I pass into the air."
Take my hand. Now tell me: flesh or tallow?
Which I am tonight, I leave to you.'

So take my hand and tell me, flesh or tallow.
Which man I am tonight I leave to you.

---

* Generic name for several species of seabird, the flesh of which is so
  saturated in oil the whole bird can be threaded with a wick and
  burnt entire

02:50: Newtyle

Of this white page, ask no more sense
than of the skies (though you may believe
the rain His tears, the wind His grief,
the snow His shredded evidence

that covers up the hill and cross,
the fallen hush, His own held breath)
but stare it down: the thawing earth
sustains a temporary gloss

from
THE EYES

a version of
Antonio Machado

Advice

My advice? To watch, and wait for the tide to turn –
wait as the beached boat waits, without a thought
for either its own waiting, or departure.
As I put it so well myself: 'The patient triumph
since life is long, and art merely a toy.'

Well – okay – supposing life is short,
and the sea never touches your little boat –
just wait, and watch, and wait, for art is long;
whatever. To be quite honest with you,
none of this is terribly important.

Chords

Perhaps, when we're half-asleep,
the same hand that sows the stars
trails across that galactic lyre . . .
the dying wave reaching our lips
as two or three true words

Dream

I woke. Was it her breath or my own
that misted up the window of my dream?
My heart's all out of time . . .
The black flame of the cypress in the orchard,
the lemon-blossom in the meadow . . .
then a tear in the clouds,
the land brightening in its lantern
of sun and rain, the sudden rainbow;
then all of it, inverted, minuscule, in each speck
of rain in her black hair!
And I let it slip away again
like a soap-bubble in the wind . . .

The Eyes

When his beloved died
he decided to grow old
and shut himself inside
the empty house, alone
with his memories of her
and the big sunny mirror
where she'd fixed her hair.
This great block of gold
he hoarded like a miser,
thinking here, at least,
he'd lock away the past,
keep one thing intact.

But around the first anniversary,
he began to wonder, to his horror,
about her eyes: *Were they brown or black,
or grey? Green? Christ! I can't say . . .*

One Spring morning, something gave in him;
shouldering his twin grief like a cross,
he shut the front door, turned into the street
and had walked just ten yards, when, from a dark close,
he caught a flash of eyes. He lowered his hat-brim
and walked on . . . *yes, they were like that; like that . . .*

Profession of Faith

God is not the sea, but of its nature:
He scatters like the moonlight on the water
or appears on the horizon like a sail.
The sea is where He wakes, or sinks to dreams.
He made the sea, and like the clouds and storms
is born of it, over and over. Thus the Creator
finds himself revived by his own creature:
he thrives on the same spirit he exhales.

I'll make you, Lord, as you made me, restore
the soul you gifted me; in time, uncover
your name in my own. Let that pure source
that pours its empty heart out to us pour
through my heart too; and let the turbid river
of every heartless faith dry up for ever.

Meditation

Is my heart asleep?
Has the dream-hive
fallen still,
the wheel that drives
the mind's red mill
slowed and slowed
to a stop, each scoop
full of only shadow?

No, my heart's awake,
perfectly awake;
it watches the horizon
for the white sail, listens
along the shoreline
of the ancient silence

Nothing

So is this magic place to die with us?
I mean that world where memory still holds
the breath of your early life:
the white shadow of first love,
that voice that rose and fell
with your own heart, the hand
you'd dream of closing in your own . . .
all those beloved burning things
that dawned on us,
lit up the inner sky?
Is this whole world to vanish when we die,
this life that we made new in our own fashion?
Have the crucibles and anvils of the soul
been working for the dust and for the wind?

from One Day's Poem

So here he is,
your man, the Modern Languages Teacher
(late occupant of the ghost-chair,
ahem, of *gaya ciencia*,
the nightingale's apprentice)
in a dark sprawl somewhere between
Andalusia and La Mancha.
Winter. A fire lit.
Outside a fine rain
swithers between mist and sleet.
Imagining myself a farmer,
I think of the good Lord astride
the tilled fields, tapping the side
of his great riddle, keeping up
the steady murmur
over the parched crops,
over the olive-groves and vineyards.
They've prayed hard
and now they can sing their hosannas:
those with new-sown wheat,
those who'll pick
the fattened olives,
those, who in their whole lives
aspire to no more luck
than enough to eat;
those who now, as ever,
put all their little silver
on one turn of the wheel,
the terrible wheel of the seasons.

In my room, brilliant
with the pearl-light
of winter, strained
through cloud and glass and rain,
I dream and meditate.
The clock
glitters on the wall,
its ticktock
drifting in and out
of my head. *Ticktock, ticktock,*
there; now I hear it.
Ticktock, ticktock, the dead click
of its mechanical heart . . .
In these towns, one fights –
oh for a second's respite! –
with those bleak hiccups
from the clock's blank face
that count out time as emptiness,
like a tailor taking his measuring-tape
to yard on yard of space.
But your hour, is it *the* hour?
Your time, friend, is it ours?
(*ticktock, ticktock*) On a day
(*ticktock*) you would say had passed
death took away
the thing that I held dearest.

Bells in the distance.

The rain drums harder
on the windowpanes.
A farmer again,
I go back to my fields of grain . . .

. . . It's getting darker:
I watch the filament
redden and glow;
I'd get more light from a match
or the moonshine.
God knows where my glasses went –
(if one had to define
the pointless search!)
amongst these reviews, old papers . . .
who'd find anything?
. . . Aha. Here we go.
New books.
I open one by Unamuno –
the pride and joy
of our Spanish revival –
no, *renaissance*, to hell
with it . . . This country dominie
has always carried the torch for you,
Rector of Salamanca.
This philosophy of yours
you call dilettantish,
just a balancing act –
Don Miguel, it's mine too.
It's water from the true source,
a downpour, then a burn, a cataract,
always alive, always fugitive . . . it's poetry,

a real thing of the heart.

But can we really build on it?
There's no foundation
in the spirit or the wind –
no anchorage, no anchor;
only the work –
our rowing or sailing
towards the shoreless ocean . . .

Henri Bergson: *The Immediate
Data of Consciousness*. Looks
like another of these French tricks . . .
This Bergson is a rogue,
Master Unamuno, true?
I'd sooner take that boy
from Königsberg
and his – how'd you put it –
salto inmortal . . .
that devilish jew
worked out free will
within his own four walls.
It's okay, I guess – every scholar
with his headache, every lunatic
wrestling with his . . .

I suppose it matters
in this short, troublesome affair
whether we're slaves or free;
but, if we're all bound for the sea,
it's all the same in the end.
God, these country backwaters!
All our idle notes and glosses
soon show up for what they are:
the yawns of Solomon . . .
no, more like Ecclesiastes:
a solitude of solitudes,
vanity of vanities . . .

. . . The rain's slacking off.
Umbrella, hat, gaberdine, galoshes . . .
Right. I'm out of here.

Paradoxes

(i)

Just as the lover's sky is bluest
the poet's muse is his alone;
the dead verse and its readership
have lives and muses of their own.
The poem we think we have *made up*
may still turn out to be our truest.

(ii)

Only in our sorrows do we live
within the heart of consciousness, the lie.
Meeting his master crying in the road,
a student took Solon to task: 'But why,
your son long in the ground, do you still grieve
if, as you say, man's tears avail him nothing?'
'Young friend,' said Solon, lifting his old head,
'I weep *because* my tears avail me nothing.'

Poem

I want neither glory
nor that, in the memory
of men, my songs survive;
but still . . . those subtle worlds,
those weightless mother-of-pearl
soap-bubbles of mine . . . I just love
the way they set off, all tarted up
in sunburst and scarlet, hover
low in the blue sky, quiver,
then suddenly pop

Poetry

In the same way that the mindless diamond keeps
one spark of the planet's early fires
trapped forever in its net of ice,
it's not love's later heat that poetry holds,
but the atom of the love that drew it forth
from the silence: so if the bright coal of his love
begins to smoulder, the poet hears his voice
suddenly forced, like a bar-room singer's – boastful
with his own huge feeling, or drowned by violins;
but if it yields a steadier light, he knows
the pure verse, when it finally comes, will sound
like a mountain spring, anonymous and serene.
Beneath the blue oblivious sky, the water
sings of nothing, not your name, not mine.

Promethean

The traveller is the aggregate of the road.
In a walled garden beside the ocean's ear
he carries his whole journey on his coat –
the hoarfrost and the coffee-smell, the dry heat
of the hay, the dog-rose, the bitter woodsmoke.
The long day's veteran, he puts a brake
on all sentiment, and waits for the slow word
to surface in his mind, as if for air.

This was my dream – and then I dreamt that time,
that quiet assassin drawing us through the days
towards our end, was just another dream . . .
And at that, I saw the gentle traveller lift
his palm to the low sun, and make a gift
of it: the Name, the Word, the ashless blaze.

Road

Traveller, your footprints are
the only path, the only track:
wayfarer, there is no way,
there is no map or Northern star,
just a blank page and a starless dark;
and should you turn round to admire
the distance that you've made today
the road will billow into dust.
No way on and no way back,
there is no way, my comrade: trust
your own quick step, the end's delay,
the vanished trail of your own wake,
wayfarer, sea-walker, Christ.

Siesta

Now that, halfway home, the fire-fish swims
between the cypress and that highest blue
into which the blind boy lately flew
in his white stone, and with the ivory poem
of the cicada ringing hollow in the elm,
let us praise the Lord –
the black print of his good hand! – who has declared
this silence in the pandemonium.

To the God of absence and of aftermath,
of the anchor in the sea, the brimming sea . . .
whose truant omnipresence sets us free
from this world, and firmly on the one true path,
with our cup of shadows overflowing, with
our hearts uplifted, heavy and half-starved,
let us honour Him who made the Void, and carved
these few words from the thin air of our faith.

Sigh

          Again
        my heart
         creaks
      on its hinge
   and with a long
           sigh
        opens on
      the arcade
          of my short
          history
         where
        the orange
     and acacia
   are flowering
   in the courtyard
          and the fountain
         sings
           then speaks
        its love-song
         to no one

from
LANDING LIGHT

Luing

When the day comes, as the day surely must,
when it is asked of you, and you refuse
to take that lover's wound again, that cup
of emptiness that is our one completion,

I'd say go here, maybe, to our unsung
innermost isle: Kilda's antithesis,
yet still with its own tiny stubborn anthem,
its yellow milkwort and its stunted kye.

Leaving the motherland by a two-car raft,
the littlest of the fleet, you cross the minch
to find yourself, if anything, now deeper
in her arms than ever – sharing her breath,

watching the red vans sliding silently
between her hills. In such intimate exile,
who'd believe the burn behind the house
the straitened ocean written on the map?

Here, beside the fordable Atlantic,
reborn into a secret candidacy,
the fontanelles reopen one by one
in the palms, then the breastbone and the brow,

aching at the shearwater's wail, the rowan
that falls beyond all seasons. One morning
you hover on the threshold, knowing for certain
the first touch of the light will finish you.

St Brides: Sea-Mail

Now they have gone
we are sunk, believe me.
Their scentless oil, so volatile
it only took one stray breath on its skin
to set it up – it was our sole
export, our currency
and catholicon.

There was a gland
below each wing, a duct
four inches or so down the throat;
though it was tiresome milking them by hand
given the rumour of their infinite
supply, and the blunt fact
of our demand.

After the cull
we'd save the carcasses,
bind the feet and fan the wings,
sew their lips up, empty out their skulls
and carry them away to hang
in one of the drying-houses,
twelve to a pole.

By Michaelmas
they'd be so light and stiff
you could lift one up by its ankle
or snap the feathers from its back like glass.
Where their eyes had been were inkwells.
We took them to the cliffs
and made our choice.

[80]

Launching them,
the trick was to 'make
a little angel': ring- and fore-
fingers tucked away, pinkie and thumb
spread wide for balance, your
middle finger hooked
under the sternum.

Our sporting myths:
the windless, perfect day
McNicol threw beyond the stac;
how, ten years on, MacFarlane met his death
to a loopback. Whatever our luck,
by sunset, they'd fill the bay
like burnt moths.

The last morning
we shuffled out for parliament
their rock was empty, and the sky clear
of every wren and fulmar and whitewing.
The wind has been so weak all year
I post this more in testament
than hope or warning.

Sliding on Loch Ogil

Remember, brother soul, that day spent cleaving
nothing from nothing, like a thrown knife?
Then there was no arriving and no leaving,
just a dream of the disintricated life –
crucified and free, the still man moving,
the balancing his work, the wind his wife.

Waking with Russell

Whatever the difference is, it all began
the day we woke up face-to-face like lovers
and his four-day-old smile dawned on him again,
possessed him, till it would not fall or waver;
and I pitched back not my old hard-pressed grin
but his own smile, or one I'd rediscovered.
Dear son, I was *mezzo del cammin*
and the true path was as lost to me as ever
when you cut in front and lit it as you ran.
See how the true gift never leaves the giver:
returned and redelivered, it rolled on
until the smile poured through us like a river.
How fine, I thought, this waking amongst men!
I kissed your mouth and pledged myself forever.

The Thread

Jamie made his landing in the world
so hard he ploughed straight back into the earth.
They caught him by the thread of his one breath
and pulled him up. They don't know how it held.
And so today I thank what higher will
brought us to here, to you and me and Russ,
the great twin-engined swaying wingspan of us
roaring down the back of Kirrie Hill

and your two-year-old lungs somehow out-revving
every engine in the universe.
All that trouble just to turn up dead
was all I thought that long week. Now the thread
is holding all of us: look at our tiny house,
son, the white dot of your mother waving.

The Forest of the Suicides
Inferno, Canto xiii

Who are these pietàs?
The shadows of ringdoves chanting, but easing nothing.
                                  Sylvia Plath, '*Winter Trees*'

Nessus was still midriver, trotting back
to the far bank, when suddenly I found
I was back in a dark wood, this time unmarked
by any path at all. I looked around.

Each barren, blood-black tree was like a plate
from a sailor's book of knots, its branches bent
and pleached and coiled as if to demonstrate
some novel and ingenious kind of torment.

In the topmost branches of those wretched trees
I saw the Snatcher build its nest; whose kin
drove Aeneas from the Strophades,
spoiled his table, and spat out his ruin.

There it squats, its human face all wrong
above its fledged gut, wide-winged, razor-clawed.
With its avian knack of mimicry, its song
is a loop-tape of the children it has tortured.

I felt so desolate, it gave me a start
to hear his voice. 'Now, friend; before we leave
stand still for just a moment, and listen hard.
This place is almost too strange to believe.'

Below the pitiful sobs and chokes and cries
lower moans were echoing through the glade,
yet I saw no one to make them. 'Master, why
do they hide from us?' I asked. 'Are they afraid?'

Then he replied: 'Break off a little spray
from any plant here: then I guarantee
things will become clearer.' I snapped away
a twig from the bush that stood closest to me.

In the trunk, a red mouth opened like a cut.
Then a voice screamed out 'Why are you tearing me?'
It was a woman's voice. Blood began to spurt
from the broken tip. 'You, are you hearing me?

When exactly did I earn *your* scorn?
Supposing I'd a heart black as a snake's,
I was a woman once, that now am thorn.
What would a little pity have set you back?'

Just in the way a split cord of green wood,
lit at one end, starts to spit and blister
at the other, so it was the words and blood
bubbled from her splintered mouth. 'Dear sister,'

my guide interrupted, 'if only my poor friend
had recalled what I had written of this hell
I know he never would have raised his hand
against you; but the truth is so incredible

I urged him on. Forgive his ignorance –
but he can make amends; just tell him who
you were, and how you came here. When he returns
to the upper world, your fame can bloom anew.'

And then the tree laughed. 'Bravo sir! Well said.
You'd spend a lifetime trying to put it worse.
In my design, that scalded beach ahead
would be reserved for the biographers.

And if it's self-improvement your friend seeks
perhaps it's courtesy you need to teach . . .
Ah. But you can see that I am weak,
and lured into a little human speech.

Very well. When I was small, I held both keys
that fitted my father's heart; which I unlocked
and locked again with such a delicate ease
he felt no turning, and he heard no click.

He desired no other confidence but mine;
nor would I permit one. I was so bound
to my splendid office that, when he resigned,
I followed. They had to dig me from the ground.

So the post remained, and I remained as true;
and, in time, I came to interview
for his successor. None of them would do
until a black shape cut the light in two

and at once I knew my ideal candidate.
But that green-eyed courtesan, that vice of courts
who had always stalked his halls and kept his gate –
the years had steeped me in her sullen arts

and my tongue grew hot with her abysmal need.
Slowly, I turned it on my second Caesar
until it seemed to him his every deed
did nothing but disgrace his predecessor.

So he left me too; but the tongue still burned away
till I sung the bright world only to estrange it,
and prophesied my end so nakedly
mere decency insisted I arrange it.

My mind, then, in its voice of reasoned harm
told me Death would broker my release
from every shame, and back into his arms;
so I made my date. It was bad advice.

But if your friend should somehow cut a path
back to the light, then tell them I betrayed
the spirit, not the letter of the oath –
by far the lesser crime in our dark trade.'

My master hissed: 'Listen – she's silent now.
Quickly, don't just throw away your chance;
ask her, if there's more you wish to know.'
I replied: 'My lord, you know the questions

I brought with me; so ask what I would ask.
I have no stomach for this conversation.'
He nodded. 'That this man may fulfil his task
and witness for you at his final station,

imprisoned soul – if you could bear to – say
just how the spirit comes to be so caught
in these terrible spasms, and if perhaps one day
it might be wrested free of its own knots.'

Long seconds passed before she spoke again.
'Remember: though these words are some relief,
the breath I draw to fill them gives a pain
beyond your knowledge. I will be brief.

The very instant that the furious soul
tears itself from the flesh, some inverse power
bundles it screaming down the sudden hole
that opens in the bed or bath or floor;

then Minos directs it to the seventh pit
where it spins down to this starless nursery
to seed wherever fortune tosses it.
There it roots, and drives up through the clay

to grow into the shape of its own anguish.
Finally, the Harpies swarm to crop
the leaves and buds – a blessing and a scourge,
since it pains us, and yet lets the pain escape.

And like you, at the final clarion,
we'll return to fish our bodies from the ground,
but never again to wear them: such is the sin
of our ingratitude. Instead, we'll drag them down

to this dark street; and here they'll stay, strung out
forever in their miserable parade –
naked and still, each hung like a white coat
on the hook of its own alienated shade.'

The Hunt

By the time he met his death
I'd counted off twelve years
and in the crossed and harrowed path
could read my whole career

the nights of circling alone
in corridors of earth
the days like paler nights, my lodestone
dying to the north

while I lived by what uncertain meat
was left from his repast
and what rainwater and bitter light
could worm in through the crust

And in that time my axe had swung
no closer to his neck
than the echo of his sullen tongue
or the hot smell of his wake

Though now and then I'd find a scrap
of gold thread in the dirt
and once, a corner of the map
she'd sewn into my shirt

I had no use for either here
being so long deranged
by the tortuous familiar
as once I'd been the strange

Then one day near the heart, making
a break in my patrol
I drained my flask and leant my aching
back against the wall

Across the way I saw a gap.
I conjured up a flame
and cupped it down twelve narrow steps
into an airless tomb

I gave the light from side to side.
The little vault unfurled
its mockery of the life I'd led
back in the upper world

The walls were lined with skinbound books
the floor with braided hair
in the corner, stuck with shite and wax
a bone table, a bone chair

On the table lay a dish of gall
and by it, for my lamp
a thighbone propping up a skull
inside, a tallow stump

I gently slid my spill into
one eye, then cut my breath
until a thin partitioned glow
strained out between the teeth

It was then my misbegotten quarry
swam up from the gloom
loitering in the darker doorway
to a second room

We shuffled close, like two old fools
and stood there for an age
trying to recollect the rules
by which we were engaged

I read no terror in his frown
no threat and no intrigue
the massive head was canted down
in pity or fatigue

so I put my hand out, hoping this
might break our dead impasse
and he had made to tender his
when my hand hit the glass

Letter to the Twins

*. . . for it is said, they went to school at Gabii, and were
well instructed in letters, and other accomplishments befitting
their birth. And they were called Romulus and Remus (from
ruma, the dug), as we had before, because they were found
sucking the wolf.*

Plutarch, *Parallel Lives*

Dear sons – for I am not, as you believed,
your uncle – forgive me now my dereliction.
In those nine months the single thought that grieved
me most was not your terrible instruction

in the works of men, the disillusionments –
Nanking and Srebrenica, Babi Yar –
you, bent above those tables of events
by whose low indices you might infer

how far you'd fallen. No, it was instead
the years you'd spend reconstituting all
the billion tedious skills of humanhood:
the infinite laws of Rome, the protocols

of every minor court and consulate –
that city that must rise up from its razed
foundations, mirrored and immaculate,
for as often as we come back to this place.

In sum, they might account it a disaster
but whatever I did, I did it as a deft
composer of the elements, the master
of all terrestrial drag and spin and heft;

look at this hand – the way it knows how light
to grip the pen, how far above the brim
to fill the cup, or hard to steer the kite,
or slowly it can travel through the flame.

More, it knows the vanity of each.
But were I to commend just one reserve
of study – one I promise that will teach
you nothing of *use,* and so not merely serve

to deepen your attachment or your debt,
where each small talent added to the horde
is doubled in its spending, and somehow yet
no more or less than its own clean reward –

it would be this: the honouring of your lover.
Learn this and she will guide you, if not home
then at least to its true memory. Then wherever
the world loses you, in her you are the same.

First, she will address you in a tongue
so secret she must close her mouth on yours.
In the curves and corners of this silent song
will lie the whole code of your intercourse.

Then, as you break, at once you understand
how the roses of her breast will draw in tight
at your touch, how that parched scrubland
between her thighs breaks open into wet

suddenly, as though you'd found the stream
running through it like a seam of milk;
know, by its tiny pulse and its low gleam
just where the pearl sits knuckled in its silk,

how that ochre-pink anemone relaxes
and unknots under your light hand and white spit;
and how that lovely mouth that has no kiss
will take the deepest you can plant in it;

and how to make that shape that boys, alas,
will know already as the sign for *gun*
yet slide it with a woman's gentleness
till you meet that other muzzle coming down.

Now, in all humility, retrace
your steps, that you might understand in full
the privilege that brought you to this place,
that let you know the break below the wool:

and as you lie there by her side, and feel
the wet snout of her womb nuzzle and lather
your fingertips – then you might recall
your mother; or her who said she was your mother.

A Fraud

I was twenty, and crossing
a field near Bridgefoot
when I saw something glossing
the toe of my boot

and bent down to spread
the bracken and dock
where a tiny wellhead
had broken the rock

It strained through the gap
as a little clear tongue
that replenished its shape
by the shape of its song

Then it spoke. It said *Son
I've no business with you.
Whatever I own
is the next fellow's due.*

*But if I'm his doom
or Castalian spring –
your directive's the same:
keep walking.*

But before it could soak
back into the stone
I dropped like a hawk
and I made it my own

and I bit its slim root
until it confessed
then swallowed its shout
in the cave of my breast

Now two strangers shiver
under one roof
the one who delivers
the promise and proof

and the one I deploy
for the poem or the kiss.
It gives me no joy
to tell you this.

The Reading

The first time I came to your wandering attention
my name was Simonides. Poets,
whose air of ingratitude forms in the womb,
have reason at least to thank me:
I invented the thing you now call the commission.
Oh – and one other frivolity
refined by Aquinas, tuned up by Bruno
and perfected by Hannibal Lecter.

All in good time. But first to the theme
of this evening's address: the reading.
It was not a good poem, if I say so myself.
As good as the fee, though, and better
than him who that day bought my praises: a man
of so little virtue to sing of
I ended up fleshing it out, as you do,
with something I'd found in the drawer –

a hymn that I'd made a while back, for the twin sons
of Leda, the Dioscuri.
At the feast he had held in his own dubious honour
the little king signed me to start;
but though they were quiet for my halfbaked encomium –
applauding like seals when I'd finished –
his guests, when I started to read from my own stuff,
returned to their wolfing and hollering.

The king, though, was silent. My lyric economies
had not, so it seemed, gone unnoticed.
When he offered me only one-half the struck price,
I made too much show of my anger
knowing, I dare say, his wrath the more just –
but right then I seemed to go deaf;
every eye turned on me, narrowed – at which point
I thought it a smart move to drop it.

However, I fixed each man's face in my mind,
each man at his rank at the table
(that trick of mine; your coupons, O my rapt listeners,
I'll have nailed by the end of this poem).
Then this. A young slave-girl ran into the hall
then right up to me, with this message:
two golden-haired boys had arrived at the gate,
and wanted to talk with me. Urgently.

I asked that I might be excused, a small boon
they were more than delighted to grant,
and took a slow stroll to the gate. I found no one.
Bloody kids. I turned back to the hall
and cursed them to heaven. Heaven replied
without hesitation or stint: a great thunderbolt
aimed not at me, but the ridgepole.
The roof groaned and splintered, sagged for a moment
then cracked, and came down on the lot of them.

After the dust and the sirens had died
the wives all came wailing and weeping
to claim what they could of their tenderised menfolk.
Alas, they were all so disfigured
no one could work out whose husband was whose.
Of course I could. *The redbeard? Just there,*
by the fire. And the scarface? The door. And the hawknose?
Poor woman: look under your feet.

I picked my way down to head of the table
and held the fixed gaze of my patron
as I knelt in the rafters and carefully counted
the rest of my fee from his purse.

The Rat

A young man wrote a poem about a rat.
It was the best poem ever written about a rat.
To read it was to ask the rat to perch
on the arm of your chair until you turned the page.
So we wrote to him, but heard nothing; we called,
and called again; then finally we sailed
to the island where he kept the only shop
and rapped his door until he opened up.

We took away his poems. Our hands shook
with excitement. We read them on lightboxes,
under great lamps. They were not much good.
So then we offered what advice we could
on his tropes and turns, his metrical comportment,
on the wedding of the word to the event,
and suggested that he might read this or that.
We said *Now: write us more poems like The Rat.*

All we got was cheek from him. Then silence.
We gave up on him. Him with his green arrogance
and ingratitude and his one lucky strike.
But today I read The Rat again. Its reek
announced it; then I saw its pisshole stare;
line by line it strained into the air.
Then it hissed. *For all the craft and clever-clever
you did not write me, fool. Nor will you ever.*

The Box

If it can stay
at its post,
cross-braced
between
the world
and the
weather
this one
will see
me out:
behold
its dark
scoured
innards,
fragrant
with tea
and rust,
its drum-tight
blown-egg feel, the cone
of air before it, wired and tense
as a lover by a telephone. Bert
Kwakkel,   my Dutch
luthier,   emptied
so much wood out of the wood
it takes no more than a dropped shoe
or a cleared throat on the hall landing
to set its little blue moan off again.
I port it to its stand. I let it
still. I contemplate it
like a skull.

A Gift

That night she called his name, not mine
    and could not call it back
I shamed myself, and thought of that blind
    girl in Kodiak

who sat out on the stoop each night
    to watch the daylight fade
and lift her child down to the gate cut
    in the palisade

and what old caution love resigned
    when through that misty stare
she passed the boy to not her bearskinned
    husband but the bear

The Wreck

But what lovers we were, what lovers,
even when it was all over –

the deadweight, bull-black wines we swung
towards each other rang and rang

like bells of blood, our own great hearts.
We slung the drunk boat out of port

and watched our unreal sober life
unmoor, a continent of grief;

the candlelight strange on our faces
like the tiny silent blazes

and coruscations of its wars.
We blew them out and took the stairs

into the night for the night's work,
stripped off in the timbered dark,

gently hooked each other on
like aqualungs, and thundered down

to mine our lovely secret wreck.
We surfaced later, breathless, back

to back, then made our way alone
up the mined beach of the dawn.

Twinflooer

Linnaea Borealis

Tho' it grows
in oor baald east
alane, it's still
sic an antrin baste
I anely find it
in dwam or dream,
an catch them
in thir lemanrie
hunkered alow
a wheesh't circle
cut clean fae
the blackie-sang
or lintie-sang
as ower a cairn,
or wirrikow
in a field o corn.
I pert the girss
an' there they are,
the shilpit pair
cried for him
wha rived a kingdom
in twa estates –
an' gently lift
the pallie, lither
bells thegither:
twa fingertips
tak'in up
the exact wecht
o nothin, licht
as the twa-fauld name
on yer ane jimp stem.

Win'-balance,
elf-cleek,
breist o silence –
a word hauf-swicked
fae the fa' o Babel,
whitever it spelt
sae slicht and nesh
it jinked the trouble,
and rode the jaw
as the broch tummel't
t' somehow waash
up here, a trick
or holy geg
like the *twa-in-yin*
breathed in the lug
o the blin'fauld halflin.

Lass, they say
oor nation's nae
words for *love*
the wiy we have
for daith, or deil.
Times ye feel
the mair wi gang
intil thon tongue –
hidden, fey
an' ayebydan –
the less wi hae
the need o ane.
And jist the same,
there's nae flooer here

aside the yin
I've here descreivit;
yet merk this pair,
strecht fae Ovid,
nailed thegither
wame to wame –
tynt in the ither,
ayont a' thocht,
a' deed, a' talk,
hauf-jyned, hauf-rift:
thir heids doverin
unner the licht
                    yock
    o the lift

---

baald – bald; *antrin* – rare, singular; *baste* – beast; *dwam* – day-
dream; *lemanrie* – sexual or illicit love; *wheesh't* – stilled; *blackie*
– blackbird; *lintie* – linnet; *cairn* – burial mound; *wirrikow* – scare-
crow, demon; *girss* – grass; *shilpit* – thin, weak; *cried* – called; *rived*
– split; *pallie* – pale; *lither* – lazy; *wecht* – weight; *licht* – light; *twa-
fauld* – two-fold; *jimp* – slender; *win'* – wind; *cleek* – hook; *swicked*
– cheated; *slicht* – slight; *nesh* – soft; *jinked* – dodged; *jaw* – wave,
breaker; *broch* – tower; *geg* – gag, joke; *twa-in-yin* – supposedly 'the
horseman's word'; *blin'fauld* – blindfolded; *halflin* – adolescent;
daith – death; *deil* – devil; *gang* – go; *fey* – doomed; *ayebydan*
– eternal; *descreivit* – described; *strecht* – straight; *wame* – belly;
tynt – lost; *ayont* – beyond; *thocht* – thought; *doverin* – nodding in
sleep; *yock* – yoke; *lift* – sky, heavens

'96

her sleek
thigh
on my
cheek

a flayed
tongue
in the wrong
head

no poem
all year
but its dumb

inverse
sow's ear
silk purse

The Light

When I reached his bed he was already blind.
Thirteen years had gone, and yet my mind
was as dark as on my ordination day.
Now I was shameless. I begged him for the light.
'Is it not taught *all* is illusory?
And still you did not guess the truth of it?
There is no light, fool. Now have you awoken?'
And he laughed, and then he left us. I was broken.

I went back to my room to pack my things,
my begging-bowl, my robe and cup; the prayer-mat
I would leave. It lay there, frayed and framed
in a square of late sun. And out of pure habit –
no, less, out of nothing, for I was nothing –
I watched myself sit down for one last time.

The Landing

Long months on the rising path
I found where I'd come in
and knew the word of heat, the breath
of air move on my skin

and saw the complex upper light
divide the middle tread
then to my left, the darker flight
that fell back to the dead

So like the ass between two bales
I stopped in the half-shade
too torn to say in which exile
the shame was better paid

And while I stood to dwell upon
my empty-handed quest
I watched the early morning sun
send down its golden ghost

It paused just on the lowest step
as if upon a hinge
then slowly drew the dark back up
like blood in a syringe

and suddenly I did not care
if I had lived or died
But then my hand fell on the lyre
that hung dead at my side

and with as plain a stroke I knew
I let each gutstring sound
and listened to the notes I drew
go echoing underground

then somewhere in the afternoon
the thrush's quick reply –
and in that instant knew I'd found
my perfect alibi

No singer of the day or night
is lucky as I am
the dark my sounding-board, the light
my auditorium

Zen Sang at Dayligaun

As aw we ken o the sternless derk
is the warld it fa's amang
aw we hae o the burn and birk
is thir broon or siller sang

Each pair o een in lift or yird
micht hae them by anither
tho' the birk chants t' nae baist or bird
nor burn tae human brither

For the lyart sang's no' staneyraw,
thon gowden sang's no' stane
an' there's nae burn or birk at aw
but jist the sang alane

dayligaun – twilight; *sternless* – starless; *derk* – dark; *birk* – birch;
siller – silver; *een* – eyes; *lift* – sky; *yird* – earth; *chants* – sings; *baist*
– beast; *lyart* – grizzled, silvered; *staneyraw* – lichen; *gowden* – golden

The White Lie

I have never opened a book in my life,
made love to a woman, picked up a knife,
taken a drink, caught the first train
or walked beyond the last house in the lane.

Nor could I put a name to my own face.
Everything we know to be the case
draws its signal colour off the sight
till what falls into that intellectual night

we tunnel into this view or another
falls as we have fallen. *Blessed Mother,*
when I stand between the sunlit and the sun
make me glass: and one night I looked down

to find the girl look up at me and through
me with such a radiant wonder, you
could not read it as a compliment
and so seek to return it. In the event

I let us both down, failing to display
more than a halfhearted opacity.
She turned her face from me, and the light stalled
between us like a sheet, a door, a wall.

But consider this: that when we leave the room,
the chair, the bookend or the picture-frame
we had frozen by desire or spent desire
is reconsumed in its estranging fire

such that, if we slipped back by a road
too long asleep to feel our human tread
we would not recognise a thing by name,
but think ourselves in Akhenaten's tomb;

then, as things ourselves, we would have learnt
we are the source, not the conducting element.
Imagine your shadow burning off the page
as the dear world and the dead word disengage –

in our detachment, we would surely offer
such offence to that Love that will suffer
no wholly isolated soul within
its sphere, it would blast straight through our skin

just as the day would flush out the rogue spark
it found still holding to its private dark.
But like our ever-present, all-wise god
incapable of movement or of thought,

no one at one with all the universe
can touch one thing; in such supreme divorce,
what earthly use are we to our lost brother
when we must stay partly lost to find each other?

Only by this – this shrewd obliquity
of speech, the broken word and the white lie,
do we check ourselves, as we might halt the sun
one degree from the meridian

then wedge it by the thickness of the book
that everything might keep the blackedged look
of things, and that there might be time enough
to die in, dark to read by, distance to love.

from
ORPHEUS

A version of Rilke's
Die Sonette an Orpheus

Leaving

Raise no stone to his memory. Just let
the rose put forth each year, for his name's sake.
Orpheus. In time, perhaps he'll take
the shape of this, and then of that – and yet

we need no other name: *Orpheus*, we say
wherever the true song is manifest.
He comes and goes. Therefore are we not blessed
if he outlasts the flowers for a few days?

But though his constant leaving is a torment,
leave he must, if we're to understand.
So even as his voice alters the moment,

he's already gone where no one can pursue;
even the lyre cannot ensnare his hands.
And yet in this defiance, he stays true . . .

Tone

Only one who's also raised
his lyre among the shades
may live to render up the praise
that cannot fail or fade.

Only one who tasted death's
own flower on his lips
can keep that tone as light as breath
beneath his fingertips.

Though its reflection starts to swim
before your failing sight:
know the image.

Only in the double realm
is the voice both infinite
and assuaged.

Horseman

Look at the sky: is there no constellation
called *The Horseman*? Because this is our song –
a beast's will, and some higher distillation
steering and braking as it's borne along.

Isn't this just our sinewy existence,
spurring ourselves on, reining ourselves back in?
Track and turning; then one touch – a new distance
opens up, and the two are one again.

But is that true? Don't they just signify
the road they take together? As it is,
they're sundered by the table and the trough.

Even their starry union is a lie.
For now, we can do nothing but insist
we read it there. And maybe that's enough.

Taste

Gooseberry, banana, pear
and apple, all the ripenesses . . .
Read it in the child's face:
the life-and-death the tongue hears

as she eats . . . This comes from far away.
What is happening to your mouth?
Where there were words, discovery
flows, all shocked out of the pith –

What we call *apple* . . . Do you dare
give it a name? This sweet-sharp fire
rising in the taste, to grow

clarified, awake, twin-sensed,
of the sun and earth, the here and the now –
the sensual joy, the whole Immense!

The Dead

Our business is with fruit and leaf and bloom.
Though they speak with more than just the season's
      tongue –
the colours that they blaze from the dark loam
all have something of the jealous tang

of the dead about them. What do we know of their part
in this, those secret brothers of the harrow,
invigorators of the soil – oiling the dirt
so liberally with their essence, their black marrow?

But here's the question: are the flower and fruit
held out to us in love, or merely thrust
up at us, their masters, like a fist?

Or are *they* the lords, asleep amongst the roots,
granting to us in their great largesse
this hybrid thing – part brute force, part mute kiss?

Dog

My dumb friend . . . You are so alone
because of us, each word and sign
we use to make this world our own –
the fraction that we should decline.

But can we point towards a scent?
You know the powers that threaten us.
You bark out when the dead are present;
you shrink back from the spell and curse.

These broken views we must pretend
form the whole and not the part.
Helping you will be difficult

and never plant me in your heart –
I'd grow too fast. But I'd guide his hand,
saying: *Here. This is Esau in his pelt.*

Horse

What shall I offer you, lord, what homage,
who gave the creatures their ear?
I remember one Spring, in Russia . . .
It was evening, and at the first star

a white horse
crossed the village square, one fetlock hobbled
for a night alone in the field . . .
And how his ticking mane exactly followed

his great heart, its high-swung
drumbeat – cantering as if that crude shackle
did not exist . . . How the fountains of his blood

leapt! That horse knew the distances – how he sang,
and listened! Your myth-cycle
was closed in him. I'll dedicate his image.

The Race

Man is the driver.
But time and speed
in the weave of forever
are twists in a thread:

what races or flies
is already over.
We're already baptised
in the endless river.

So boys, don't waste
your courage on time-
trials, or test-flights –

all these are at rest:
darkness and light;
the book and the bloom.

Breath

Breath, you invisible poem –
pure exchange, sister to silence,
being and its counterbalance,
rhythm wherein I become,

ocean I accumulate
by stealth, by the same slow wave;
thriftiest of seas . . . Thief
of the whole cosmos! What estates,

what vast spaces have already poured
through my lungs? The four winds
are like daughters to me.

So do you know me, air, that once sailed
    through me?
You, that were once the leaf and rind
of my every word?

Anemone

In the meadow the anemone
is creaking open to the dawn.
By noon, the sky's polyphony
will flood her white lap till she drowns.

The tiny muscle in her star
is tensed to open to the All,
yet the daylight's blast so deafens her
she barely heeds the sunset's call

or finds the willpower to refurl
her petal-edges – her, the power
and will of how many other worlds!

In our violence, we outlive her.
But which new life will see *us* flower
and face the skies, as true receivers?

The Ball

What happened to that little brotherhood,
lords of the scattered gardens of the city?
We were all so shy, I never understood
how we hooked up in the first place; like the lamb

with the scroll that spoke, we too spoke in silence.
It seemed when we were happy it was no one's;
whose ball *was* it? In all the anxiety
of that last summer, it melted in the scrum:

the street leaned like a stage-set, the traffic
rolled around us, like huge toys; nobody
knew us. What was real in that All?

Nothing. Just the ball. Its glorious arc.
Not even the kids . . . But sometimes one, already
fading, stepped below it as it fell.

The Passing

Be ahead of all departure; learn to act
as if, like the last winter, it was all over.
For among the winters, one is so exact
that wintering it, your heart will last for ever.

Die, die through Eurydice – that you might pass
into the pure accord, praising the more, singing
the more; amongst the waning, be the glass
that shatters in the sound of its own ringing.

Be; and at the same time know the state
of non-being, the boundless inner sky,
that this time you might fully honour it.

Take all of nature, its one vast aggregate –
jubilantly multiply it by
the nothing of yourself, and clear the slate.

The Flowers

Consider the flowers: true only to the earth
yet we lend them a fate, from the borders of fate,
and supervise their fadings, their little deaths.
How right that we should author their regret:

everything rises – and yet we trudge along,
laying our heavy selves upon the world.
What wearisome teachers we are for things!
While the Earth dreams on in its eternal childhood.

But if someone took them into infinite sleep,
lay down with them . . . how lightly he would waken
to the different day, out of the common deep –

or perhaps he'd stay: stay until they weakened
and took him in as one of their own kind,
a meadow-brother, a breath inside the wind.

The Drinking Fountain

O tireless giver, holy cataract,
conductor of the inexhaustible One –
your clear tongue, lifting through the mask of stone
you hold before your face . . . Behind you, aqueducts

vanish into the distance. From the Apennine
foothills, through the wheat fields and the graveyards,
they bear the sacred utterance, the words
that arrive for ever, blackening your chin

to fall into the basin that lies rapt
to your constant murmur, like a sleeping ear.
Marmoreal circumstance. Listening rock.

An ear of Earth's, so she only really talks
to herself. So when we're filling up our pitcher,
it feels to her that someone interrupts.

The Cry

The call of one lone bird can make us cry –
whatever sounds just once, then dies away.
But listen: beyond the mere sound of their play,
those yelling kids beneath the open sky –

they cry the *chance!* They hammer every scream
like a wedge into the black interstices
of the world – those cracks where only the bird-cries
can pass clean through, the way men do in dreams.

O, where are we now? Freer and freer,
like kites torn from their lines, we loop and race
in the middle air . . . Our tattered hems snicker

like lunatics . . . O lord, make one great choir
of all the criers, so they wake as one voice,
one current, carrying both the head and lyre!

Time

Is there really such thing as time-the-destroyer?
When will it shatter the tower on the rock?
When will that low demiurge overpower
this heart, that runs only to heaven's clock?

Are we really so fragile, so easily broken
as fate wants to prove us, or have us believe?
Is the infinite life that our childhood awakened
torn up by the roots, and then thrown in the grave?

Look how the ghosts of impermanence slide
straight through the mind of the open receiver
again and again, like smoke through a tree.

Among the Eternal – wherein we reside
as that which we truly are, the urgent, the strivers –
we still count; as their means, as their Earth-agency.

Being

Silent comrade of the distances,
Know that space dilates with your own breath;
ring out, as a bell into the Earth
from the dark rafters of its own high place –

then watch what feeds on you grow strong again.
Learn the transformations through and through:
what in your life has most tormented you?
If the water's sour, turn it into wine.

Our senses cannot fathom this night, so
be the meaning of their strange encounter;
at their crossing, be the radiant centre.

And should the world itself forget your name
say this to the still earth: *I flow*.
Say this to the quick stream: *I am*.

from
RAIN

Two Trees

One morning, Don Miguel got out of bed
with one idea rooted in his head:
to graft his orange to his lemon tree.
It took him the whole day to work them free,
lay open their sides, and lash them tight.
For twelve months, from the shame or from the fright
they put forth nothing; but one day there appeared
two lights in the dark leaves. Over the years
the limbs would get themselves so tangled up
each bough looked like it gave a double crop,
and not one kid in the village didn't know
the magic tree in Miguel's patio.

The man who bought the house had had no dream
so who can say what dark malicious whim
led him to take his axe and split the bole
along its fused seam, then dig two holes.
And no, they did not die from solitude;
nor did their branches bear a sterile fruit;
nor did their unhealed flanks weep every spring
for those four yards that lost them everything,
as each strained on its shackled root to face
the other's empty, intricate embrace.
They were trees, and trees don't weep or ache or shout.
And trees are all this poem is about.

The Error

As the bird is to the air
and the whale is to the sea
so man is to his dream.

His world is just the glare
of the world's utility
returned by his eye-beam.

Each self-reflecting mind
is in this manner destined
to forget its element,

and this is why we find
however deep we listen
that the skies are silent.

The Swing

The swing was picked up for the boys,
for the here-and-here-to-stay
and only she knew why it was
I dug so solemnly

I spread the feet two yards apart
and hammered down the pegs
filled up the holes and stamped the dirt
around its skinny legs

I hung the rope up in the air
and fixed the yellow seat
then stood back that I might admire
my handiwork complete

and saw within its frail trapeze
the child that would not come
of what we knew had two more days
before we sent it home

I know that there is nothing here
no venue and no host
but the honest fulcrum of the hour
that engineers our ghost

the bright sweep of its radar-arc
is all the human dream
handing us from dark to dark
like a rope over a stream

But for all the coldness of my creed
for all those I denied
for all the others she had freed
like arrows from her side

for all the child was barely here
and for all that we were over
I could not weigh the ghosts we are
against those we deliver

I gave the empty seat a push
and nothing made a sound
and swung between two skies to brush
her feet upon the ground

Why Do You Stay Up So Late?

for Russ

I'll tell you, if you really want to know:
remember that day you lost two years ago
at the rockpool where you sat and played the jeweller
with all those stones you'd stolen from the shore?
Most of them went dark and nothing more,
but sometimes one would blink the secret colour
it had locked up somewhere in its stony sleep.
This is how you knew the ones to keep.

So I collect the dull things of the day
in which I see some possibility
but which are dead and which have the surprise
I don't know, and I've no pool to help me tell –
so I look at them and look at them until
one thing makes a mirror in my eyes
then I paint it with the tear to make it bright.
This is why I sit up through the night.

The Circle
for Jamie

My boy is painting outer space,
and steadies his brush-tip to trace
the comets, planets, moon and sun
and all the circuitry they run

in one great heavenly design.
But when he tries to close the line
he draws around his upturned cup,
his hand shakes, and he screws it up.

The shake's as old as he is, all
(thank god) his body can recall
of that hour when, one inch from home,
we couldn't get the air to him;

and though today he's all the earth
and sky for breathing-space and breath
the whole damn troposphere can't cure
the flutter in his signature.

But Jamie, nothing's what we meant.
The dream is taxed. We all resent
the quarter bled off by the dark
between the bowstring and the mark

and trust to Krishna or to fate
to keep our arrows halfway straight.
But the target also draws our aim –
our will and nature's are the same;

we are its living word, and not
a book it wrote and then forgot,
its fourteen-billion-year-old song
inscribed in both our right and wrong –

so even when you rage and moan
and bring your fist down like a stone
on your spoiled work and useless kit,
you just can't help but broadcast it:

look at the little avatar
of your muddy water-jar
filling with the perfect ring
singing under everything.

The Lie

As was my custom, I'd risen a full hour
before the house had woken to make sure
that everything was in order with The Lie,
his drip changed and his shackles all secure.

I was by then so practised in this chore
I'd counted maybe thirteen years or more
since last I'd felt the urge to meet his eye.
Such, I liked to think, was our rapport.

I was at full stretch to test some ligature
when I must have caught a ragged thread, and tore
his gag away; though as he made no cry,
I kept on with my checking as before.

Why do you call me The Lie? he said. I swore:
it was a child's voice. I looked up from the floor.
The dark had turned his eyes to milk and sky
and his arms and legs were all one scarlet sore.

He was a boy of maybe three or four.
His straps and chains were all the things he wore.
Knowing I could make him no reply
I took the gag before he could say more

and put it back as tight as it would tie
and locked the door and locked the door and locked the door

Correctives

The shudder in my son's left hand
he cures with one touch from his right,
two fingertips laid feather-light
to still his pen. He understands

the whole man must be his own brother
for no man is himself alone;
though some of us have never known
the one hand's kindness to the other.

Song for Natalie 'Tusja' Beridze

O Natalie, O TBA, O Tusja: I had long assumed the
terrorist's balaclava that you sport on the cover of *Annulé* –
which was, for too long, the only image of you I
possessed – was there to conceal some ugliness or deformity
    or perhaps merely spoke (and here, I hoped against
hope) of a young woman struggling
    with a crippling shyness. How richly this latter theory
has been confirmed by my Googling!

O who is this dark angel with her unruly Slavic
eyebrows ranged like two duelling pistols, lightly sweating in
the pale light of the TTF screen?
    O behold her shaded, infolded concentration, her
heartbreakingly beautiful face so clearly betraying the true
focus of one not merely content – as, no doubt, were others
at the Manöver Elektronische Festival in Wien –
    to hit *play* while making some fraudulent correction to a
volume slider
    but instead deep in the manipulation of some complex
real-time software, such as Ableton Live, MAX/MSP or
Supercollider.

O Natalie, how can I pay tribute to your infinitely
versatile blend of Nancarrow, Mille Plateaux, Venetian
Snares, Xenakis, Boards of Canada and Nobukazu Takemura
    to say nothing of those radiant pads – so strongly
reminiscent of the mid-century bitonal pastoral of Charles
Koechlin in their harmonic bravura –
    or your fine vocals, which, while admittedly limited in
range and force, are nonetheless so much more affecting

than the affected Arctic whisperings of those
interchangeably dreary
    Stinas and Hannes and Björks, being in fact far closer in
spirit to a kind of glitch-hop Blossom Dearie?

I have also deduced from your staggeringly ingenious
employment of some pretty basic wavetables
    that unlike many of your East European counterparts,
all your VST plug-ins, while not perhaps the best available
    probably all have a legitimate upgrade path – indeed I
imagine your entire DAW as pure as the driven snow, and not
in any way buggy or virusy
    which makes me love you more, demonstrating as it does
an excess of virtue given your country's well-known talent for
software piracy.

Though I should confess that at times I find your habit
of maxxing
    the range with those bat-scaring ring-modulated
sine-bursts and the more distressing psychoacoustic properties
of phase inversion in the sub-bass frequencies somewhat taxing
    you are nonetheless as beautiful as the mighty Boards
themselves in your shameless organicising of the code,
    as if you had mined those saws and squares and ramps
straight from the Georgian motherlode.

O Natalie – I forgive you everything, even your
catastrophic adaptation of those lines from 'Dylan's' already
shite
    Do Not Go Gentle Into That Good Night

in the otherwise magnificent 'Sleepwalkers', and when
you open up those low-
        pass filters in what sounds like a Minimoog emulation
they seem to open in my heart also.

O Natalie: know that I do not, repeat, do *not* imagine
you with a reconditioned laptop bought with a small grant
from the local arts cooperative in the cramped back bedroom
of an ex-communist apartment block in Tbilisi or Kutaisi
        but at the time of writing your biographical details are
extremely hazy;
        however, I feel sure that by the time this poem sees the
light of day Wire magazine will have honoured you with a far
more extensive profile than you last merited when
mention of that wonderful Pharrell remix
        was sandwiched between longer pieces on the notorious
Kyoto-based noise guitarist Idiot O'Clock, and a woman
called Sonic Pleasure who plays the housebricks.

However this little I have gleaned: firstly, that you are
married to Thomas Brinkmann, whose records are boring
– an opinion I held long before love carried me away –
        and secondly, that TBA
        is not an acronym, as I had first assumed, but Georgian
for 'lake' – in which case it probably has a silent 't', like
'Tbilisi', and so is pronounced *baa*
        which serendipitously rhymes a bit with my only other
word of Georgian, being your term for 'mother' which is
'dada', or possibly 'father' which is 'mama'.

I doubt we will ever meet, unless this somehow reaches
you on the wind;
    we will never sit with a glass of tea in your local
wood-lined café while I close-question you on how you
programmed that unbelievably great snare on 'Wind',
    of such brickwalled yet elastic snap it sounded exactly
like a 12" plastic ruler bent back and released with great
violence on the soft gong
    of a large white arse, if not one white for long.

    But Natalie – Tusja, if I may – I will not pretend I hold
much hope for us, although I have, I confess, worked up my
little apologia:
    I am not like those other middle-agey I-
    DM enthusiasts: I have none of their hangdog pathos,
my geekery is the dirty secret that it should be
    and what I lack in hair, muscle-tone and rugged good
looks I make up for with a dry and ready wit . . . but I know
that time and space conspire against me.

    At least, my dear, let me wish you the specific best:
    may you be blessed
    with the wonderful instrument you deserve, fitted –
at the time of writing – with a 2 GHz dual-core Intel chip
and enough double-pumped DDR2 RAM for the most
CPU-intensive processes;
    then no longer will all those gorgeous acoustic spaces

be accessible only via an offline procedure involving a freeware convolution reverb and an imperfectly recorded impulse response of the Concertgebouw made illegally with a hastily erected stereo pair and an exploded crisp bag

for I would have all your plug-ins run in real-time, in the blameless zero-latency heaven of the 32-bit floating-point environment, with no buffer-glitch or freeze or dropout or lag;

I would also grant you a golden midi controller, of such responsiveness, smoothness of automation, travel and increment

that you would think it a transparent intercessor, a mere copula, and feel machine and animal suddenly blent.

This I wish you as I leave Inverkeithing and Fife

listening to *Trepa N* for the two hundred and thirty-fourth time in my life

with every hair on my right arm rising in non-fascistic one-armed salutation

towards Natalie, Tba, my Tusja, and all the mountain lakes of her small nation.

The Story of the Blue Flower

My boy was miles away, yes, I admit it,
but the place was empty, my lines of sight were good
and besides, such things were unknown in this town –
though none of this did much to comfort me
when I raised my head to see the two of them
stop his mouth and lift him from the swing
with a kind of goblin-like economy
and hurry off his little flexing torso
to the orange van laid up behind the gate.
And that was that. I knew it was all over.

I was in the northeast corner of the park,
waist-deep in the ferns where I'd been hunting
the small black ball we'd lost the day before.
I howled, of course I did, but nothing came.
I only knew that failure of the will
as when you wake inside your sleeping body
and find you have no choice but to fall back
to your dead dream again. And so I did.
I fell to somewhere far below the earth
beside the roar of blind and nameless rivers.

Night followed night. I'd been a lifetime there
when through the dark I saw a pale blue star
I half-recalled, like a detail from a book
I'd loved and feared as a child. Then weeds, and sky
and all was bright and terrible again
except that I was fixed on the blue flower,
like one of those they say are always with us
whose silent glamour makes invisible.
Either way, I was suddenly on my knees
filling and filling my mouth with its bad leaves.

I can call back nothing of the missing hours
but vague things, between image and sensation:
a black wind, a white knife in my head,
and an awful centrifugal déjà vu
slowly slowing to the place I knew
as home, and the boy safe, and the boy safe.
They found them wandering the park at dusk
crying like two wee birds, their crimson faces
streaming with the jellies of their eyes
and no story they could tell of anything.

Parallax

the unbearable lightness of being no one
Slavoj Žižek

The moon lay silent on the sea
as on a polished shelf
rolling out and rolling out
its white path to the self

But while I stood illumined
like a man in his own book
I knew I was encircled by
the blindspot of its look

Because the long pole of my gaze
was all that made it turn
I was the only thing on earth
the moon could not discern

At such unearthly distance
we are better overheard.
The moon was in my mouth. It said
A million eyes. One word

for Michael Longley

The Day

for Maureen and Gus

Life is no miracle. Its sparks flare up
invisibly across the night. The heart
kicks off again where any rock can cup
some heat and wet and hold it to its star.
We are not chosen, just too far apart
to know ourselves the commonplace we are,

as precious only as the gold in the sea:
nowhere and everywhere. So be assured
that even in our own small galaxy
there is another town whose today-light
won't reach a night of ours till Kirriemuir
is nothing but a vein of hematite

where right now, two – say hairless, tall and dark,
but still as like ourselves as makes no odds –
push their wheeled contraptions through the park
under the red-leafed trees and the white birds.
Last week, while sceptic of their laws and gods
they made them witness to their given word.

They talk, as we do now, of the Divide;
but figure that who else should think of this
might also find some warmth there, and decide
to set apart one minute of the day
to dream across the parsecs, the abyss,
a kind of cosmic solidarity.

'But it's still so sad,' he says. 'Think: all of us
as cut off as the living from the dead.
It's the size that's all wrong here. The emptiness.'
She says, 'Well it's a miracle I found you
in all this space and dust.' He turns his head
and smiles the smile she recognized him through.

'I wasn't saying differently. It's just –
the biggest flashlight we could put together
is a match struck in the wind out here. We're lost.'
'I only meant – there's no more we traverse
than the space between us. The sun up there's no farther.
We're each of us a separate universe.

We talk, make love, we sleep in the same bed –
but no matter what we do, you can't be me.
We only dream this place up in one head.'
'Thanks for that . . . You're saying that because
the bed's a light-year wide, or might as well be,
I'm even lonelier than I thought I was?'

'No . . . just that it's why we have this crap
of souls and gods and ghosts and afterlives.
Not to . . . *bridge eternity*. Just the gap' –
she measures it – 'from here to here.' 'Tough call.
Death or voodoo. Some alternatives.'
'There's one more. That you trust me with it *all*.'

The wind is rising slowly through the trees;
the dark comes, and the first moon shows; they turn
their lighter talk to what daft ceremonies
the people of that star – he points to ours –
might make, what songs and speeches they might learn,
how they might dress for it, their hats and flowers,

and what signs they exchange (as stars might do,
their signals meeting in the empty bands)
to say *even in this nothingness I found you;
I was lucky in the timing of my birth*.
They stare down at their own five-fingered hands
and the rings that look like nothing on that earth.

Phantom

i.m. M.D.

I

The night's surveillance. Its heavy breathing
even in the day it hides behind.
Enough is enough for anyone, and so
you crossed your brilliant room, threw up the shade
to catch the night pressed hard against the glass,
threw up the sash and looked it in the eye.
Yet it did not stare you out of your own mind
or roll into the room like a black fog,
but sat there at the sill's edge, patiently,
like a priest into whose hearing you confessed
every earthly thing that tortured you.
While you spoke, it reached into the room
switching off the mirrors in their frames
and undeveloping your photographs;
it gently drew a knife across the threads
that tied your keepsakes to the things they kept;
it slipped into a thousand murmuring books
and laid a black leaf next to every white;
it turned your desk-lamp off, then lower still.
Soon there was nothing in that soundless dark
but, afloat on nothing, one white cup
which somehow had escaped your inventory.
The night bent down, and as a final kindness
placed it in your hands so you'd remember
to halt and stoop and drink when the time came
in that river whose name was now beyond you
as was, you found indifferently, your own.

II

Zurbarán's *St Francis in Meditation*
is west-lit, hooded, kneeling, tight in his frame;
his hands are joined, both in supplication
and to clasp the old skull to his breast.
This he is at pains to hold along
the knit-line of the parietal bone
the better, I would say, to feel the teeth
of the upper jaw gnaw into his sternum.
His face is tilted upwards, heavenwards,
while the skull, in turn, beholds his upturned face.
I would say that Francis' eyes are closed
but this is guesswork, since they are occluded
wholly by the shadow of his cowl,
for which we read the larger dark he claims
beyond the local evening of his cell.
But I would say the fetish-point, the *punctum*,
is not the skull, the white cup of his hands
or the frayed hole in the elbow of his robe,
but the tiny batwing of his open mouth
and its vowel, the *ah* of revelation, grief
or agony, but in this case I would say
there is something in the care of its depiction
to prove that we arrest the saint mid-speech.
I would say something had passed between
the man and his interrogated night.
I would say his words are not his words.
I would say the skull is working him.

III

(Or to put it otherwise: consider this
pinwheel of white linen, at its heart
a hollow, in the hollow a small hole.
We cannot say or see whether the hole
passes through the cloth, or if the cloth
darkens itself – by which I mean *gives rise*
to it, the black star at its heart,
and hosts it as a mere emergent trait
of its own intricate infolded structure.
Either way, towards the framing edge
something else is calling into question
the linen's own materiality
and the folds depicted are impossible.)

after Alison Watt: 'Breath'

IV

Zurbarán knew he could guarantee
at least one fainting fit at the unveiling
if he arranged the torch- or window-light
to echo what he'd painted in the frame.
This way, to those who first beheld the saint,
the light that fell on him seemed literal.
In the same way I might have you read these words
on a black moon, in a forest after midnight,
a thousand miles from anywhere your plea
for hearth or water might be understood
and have you strike one match, and then another –
not to light these rooms, or to augment
what little light they shed upon themselves
but to see the kind of dark I laid between them.

V

We come from nothing and return to it.
It lends us out to time, and when we lie
in silent contemplation of the void
they say we feel it contemplating us.
This is wrong, but who could bear the truth.
We are ourselves the void in contemplation.
We are its only nerve and hand and eye.
There is something vast and distant and enthroned
with which you are one and continuous,
staring through your mind, staring and staring
like a black sun, constant, silent, radiant
with neither love nor hate nor apathy
as we have no human name for its regard.
Your thought is the bright shadows that it makes
as it plays across the objects of the earth
or such icons of them as your mind has forged.
The book in sunlight or the tree in rain
bursts at its touch into a blaze of signs.
But when the mind rests and the dark light stills,
the tree will rise untethered to its station
between earth and heaven, the open book
turn runic and unreadable again,
and if a word then rises to our lips
we speak it on behalf of everything.

VI

For one whole year, when I lay down, the eye
looked through my mind uninterruptedly
and I knew a peace like nothing breathing should.
I was the no one that I was in the dark womb.
One night when I was lying in meditation
the I-Am-That-I-Am-Not spoke to me
in silence from its black and ashless blaze
in the voice of Michael Donaghy the poet.
It had lost his lightness and his gentleness
and took on that plain cadence he would use
when he read out from the *Iliad* or the *Táin*.

Your eye is no eye but an exit wound.
Mind has fired through you into the world
the way a hired thug might unload his gun
through the silk-lined pocket of his overcoat.
And even yet the dying world maintains
its air of near-hysteric unconcern
like a stateroom on a doomed ship, every
table, chair and trinket nailed in place
against the rising storm of its unbeing.
If only you had known the storm was you.

Once this place was wholly free of you.
Before life there was futureless event
and as the gases cooled and thinned and gathered
time had nothing to regret its passing
and everywhere lay lightly upon space

as daylight on the world's manifest.
Then matter somehow wrenched itself around
to see – or rather just in time to miss –
the infinite laws collapse, and there behold
the perfect niche that had been carved for it.

It made an eye to look at its fine home,
but there, within its home, it saw its death;
and so it made a self to look at death,
but then within the self it saw its death;
and so it made a soul to look at self,
but then within the soul it saw its death;
and so it made a god to look at soul,
and god could not see death within the soul
for god was death. In making death its god
the eye had lost its home in finding it.
We find this everywhere the eye appears.
Were there design, this would have been the flaw.

VII

The voice paused; and when it resumed
it had softened, and I heard the smile in it.

Donno, I can't keep this bullshit up.
I left this message planted in your head
like a letter in a book you wouldn't find
till I was long gone. Look – do this for me:
just plot a course between the Orphic oak
and fuck 'em all if they can't take a joke
and stick to it. Avoid the fancy lies
by which you would betray me worse than looking
the jerk that you're obliged to now and then.
A shame unfelt is no shame, so a man's
can't outlive him. Not that I ever worried.
Take that ancient evening, long before
my present existential disadvantage,
in Earl's Court Square with Maddy, you and Eva,
when I found those giant barcodes on the floor
and did my drunken hopscotch up and down them
while the artist watched in ashen disbelief . . .
Oh, I was always first to jump; but just because
I never got it with the gravity.
I loved the living but I hated life.
I got sick of trying to make them all forgive me
when no one found a thing to be forgiven,
sick of my knee-jerk apologies
to every lampstand that I blundered into.
Just remember these three things for me:

always take a spoon – it might rain soup;
it's as strange to be here once as to return;
and there's nothing at all between the snow and the
roses.
And don't let them misread those poems of mine
as the jeux d'esprit I had to dress them as
to get them past myself. And don't let pass
talk of my saintliness, or those attempts
to praise my average musicianship
beyond its own ambitions: music for dancers.
All I wanted was to keep the drum
so tight it was lost under their feet,
the downbeat I'd invisibly increased,
my silent augmentation of the One –
the cup I'd filled brimful . . . then even above the brim!
Nor you or I could read that line aloud
and still keep it together. But that's my point:
what kind of twisted ape ends up believing
the rushlight of his little human art
truer than the great sun on his back?
I knew the game was up for me the day
I stood before my father's corpse and thought
If I can't get a poem out of this *. . .*
Did you think any differently with mine?

He went on with his speech, but soon the eye
had turned on him once more, and I'd no wish
to hear him take that tone with me again.
I closed my mouth and put out its dark light.
I put down Michael's skull and held my own.

[167]

Rain

I love all films that start with rain:
rain, braiding a windowpane
or darkening a hung-out dress
or streaming down her upturned face;

one big thundering downpour
right through the empty script and score
before the act, before the blame,
before the lens pulls through the frame

to where the woman sits alone
beside a silent telephone
or the dress lies ruined on the grass
or the girl walks off the overpass,

and all things flow out from that source
along their fatal watercourse.
However bad or overlong
such a film can do no wrong,

so when his native twang shows through
or when the boom dips into view
or when her speech starts to betray
its adaptation from the play,

I think to when we opened cold
on a starlit gutter, running gold
with the neon of a drugstore sign
and I'd read into its blazing line:

forget the ink, the milk, the blood –
all was washed clean with the flood
we rose up from the falling waters
the fallen rain's own sons and daughters

and none of this, none of this matters.